INDIE AUTHOR CONFIDENTIAL 14

SECRETS NO ONE WILL TELL YOU ABOUT BEING A WRITER

M.L. RONN

Special thank you to the following people on Patreon who supported this book: Matty Dalrymple, BB Dee, Michael Guishard, Jon Howard, Sheila Klein, Olivia Williams, and Ryan Zee.

Some links in this book contain affiliate links. If you purchase books and services through these links, I receive a small commission at no cost to you. You are under no obligation to use these links, but thank you if you do!

For more helpful writing tips and advice, subscribe to the Author Level Up YouTube channel: www.youtube.com/authorlevelup.

CONTENTS

ABOUT THIS SERIES

This isn't your typical writing self-help book. This series is a compilation of lessons learned from an indie author trying to walk the path to success. Follow author M.L. Ronn (Michael La Ronn) as he navigates what it means to master the craft of writing, marketing, and running a profitable publishing business. Learn from his successes and failures, and learn about things that most successful authors only talk about behind the scenes.

To read all the collected volumes of this series in an anthology, visit www.authorlevelup.com/confidential.

INTRODUCTION

I have found myself thinking about mindset a lot this quarter.

We all go through seasons in our lives. In my case, I have had seasons of immense productivity, seasons of rest and relaxation, seasons of trials and tribulations, and seasons of self-unawareness and self-awareness.

I find that I never quite know what the next season will be or exactly when it will spring into my consciousness. As self-aware as I try to be, I usually don't pick up that a season has changed until several weeks or months after it happens. Then, I begin introspection to figure out what the change was, why it happened, and why it is potentially meaningful for me at this time in my life.

I shared in previous volumes that the past year has been challenging for me. It hasn't been the most productive season in my life, though it has been minimally productive. While I didn't stop writing altogether, I had to step away for a while and accept reduced output for most of the year. Fortunately, the worst of the personal issues appear to be behind me.

Something I learned during this year is that I don't handle stress well. At least, not as well as I should. I'm the sort of person who always has to be doing something and moving toward a goal. At times, I have saddled myself with too many responsibilities. For this reason, I have pulled back on my responsibilities so I can focus on the things that matter. This proved to be a smart decision that benefited my overall health, but it didn't eliminate the stress from my life. It took some dire personal circumstances with both my and my wife's health to help me see that the methods I used to cope with stress that helped me up until this point in my life weren't actually helpful.

I've always been the type of person who deals with his problems by working through them. This is a protective mechanism. I bury myself in new work and take on more responsibility to serve the people in my life better, but I don't do a good job of taking care of myself.

As I move into this next season of reflection, I've been thinking about what I can do to reverse that.

How can I manage stress better? How can I take better care of myself? How can I address problems differently than I have in the past that will still achieve the same outcomes, but in a healthier way? These are things I'm thinking about this quarter, and I believe the best way to address them is through mindset.

I don't like to do mindset work and then forget about it. It's important to me that any work I do on myself is meaningful and practical. Otherwise, it's not useful.

I also keep my guard up when I work on my mindset. I've said for a long time that there are three types of advice: advice that's meant for you, advice that's not meant for you, and advice that you're not ready for yet. There's a lot of advice that I wasn't ready for up to this point, but I am now.

In the past, the advice I sought was related to productivity and being more effective in my personal and professional lives. I was relentless about controlling the world around me to get the results I wanted. When you are building a writing career, raising a young family, working full time, and attending law school classes in the evenings (just to name a few responsibilities), then order and control are paramount.

If you aren't organized, you just sleepwalk through your life. I've done it. I know how it is. When you're organized, you at least have the illusion of control. You never really have control because life is complicated and things happen, but I have always been a fan of the mantra "Fortune favors the prepared mind." Therefore, it was my goal these past ten years to discover how best to become a prepared mind.

Much of the advice and mindset shifts I've learned have become unconscious, and I do them without having to think about them. For example, it's no trouble for me to write a novel anymore. It's no trouble to manage my book portfolio or determine what new skills I need to succeed. When I want something, I make a plan, chart a path, and go after it. I always know just what to do and when something isn't working. I chalk that up to years of experience, trial and error, and deep work on myself.

But what about my emotions? What about the "feel" of life? That, I haven't worked on so much.

During this season, it's my responsibility to start sorting this stuff out so that I can become a more balanced human being. I love being prepared, and I should not have to worry about that anymore moving forward. So, I can relax a little.

While you'll still have the usual *Indie Author Confidential* fare in this issue, you might see me waxing just a little more philosophical than I usually do. That's how seasons of life go.

My Core Strategic Priorities

As a refresher, my mission is to create content that entertains and/or educates my audience, preferably both, and to remain nimble in an ever-changing industry. I do this by focusing on three strategic priorities:

•Become a world-class content creator
•Become a technology and data-driven writer
•Become the writer of the future (looking forward)

What's in This Volume

In the Become a Writing Master section, I talk about breakthrough understandings in mindfulness, a short story conundrum, and lessons from Dean Koontz.

In the Become a Technology and Data-Driven Writer section, I revisit my annual expenses, switch cloud storage providers, and muse on the current state of AI art generators.

In the Looking Forward section, I look back at where I was this time last year, five years ago, and ten years ago.

In any case, I hope you enjoy this volume.

--M.L. Ronn
Des Moines, Iowa
July 31, 2023

BECOME A WRITING MASTER

WHAT IT MEANS TO BE A MASTER

I've defined my strategic priority of becoming a writing master, but what does that really mean? I realized I should define the term better.

A "master" is a writer with three world-class skills: writing, productivity, and people skills.

At least, that's *my* definition of a master. Your definition may vary.

Writing Skills

First, a master must be a master writer. This is perhaps the most obvious point, but we should be specific about what a "master" of writing looks like. For me, Dean Koontz, Nora Roberts, Michael Crichton, James Patterson, Ken Follett, Danielle Steel, and that ilk of writers are who I consider to be masters. There are many more. Though their styles vary widely, they have many commonalities. They're the caliber of writer I aspire to be.

We can break "writing" skills into three categories:

- Characters
- Story
- Style

While there are many, many elements to novel writing, I argue that these are the only elements that truly matter.

Characters. The masters create outstanding characters. Whether that character is a main character, supporting character, or minor character, they jump off the page and dazzle you from the moment they enter the story. The masters create characters that are instantly relatable, even if they are doing things that the average reader has never done. They're relatable even if they come from a background that the reader themselves cannot relate to. This is an art and a science.

Story. The masters are also masters at writing engaging stories. They are *not* so much masters of telling *believable* stories. In fact, the masters anger readers more often than they satisfy them. If I had a dime for every time I read a review from a reader who praised a master's books but complained about their plotting, I would be the richest man in the history of the world. But that's the secret: the masters have figured out that they just have to tell stories with intriguing premises. The actual events of the story don't have to be coherent; they must only be minimally so. They must be enough for readers to suspend their disbelief. If you can get readers to suspend their disbelief and make it to the end of the novel, then you have won. The readers who loved the book will sing its praises to their friends, and the readers who hated it will bitch about it online and increase the sales of your book possibly more than the readers who loved it.

Style. The masters are the best practitioners of writing style in the history of writing. Their voice oozes from the page. I can pick up a John Grisham novel blind and instantly know it's Grisham from the first paragraph. This is true with the other masters.

Every master has two or three distinctive aspects of their style. When married with character and story, these elements keep readers turning the page.

A trademark of Stephen King's style is his verbosity. It frustrates some readers, but his true fans love it.

Dean Koontz's calling card is his unbelievably rich yet down-to-earth vocabulary. Sometimes I think the man uses words in ways that God Himself didn't even think of.

Nora Roberts's calling card is her simple, yet heartfelt way of telling stories and getting inside characters' heads.

I could go on.

When I think about becoming a writing master, I think about these three elements. What does peak character, story, and style look like for me, and how can I take steps every day to move toward that?

For characters, it's critical for me to continue studying the masters and practicing the techniques they use to make their characters relatable. Relatable is the key word. No matter who the character is or what they're doing, how can I make them more relatable? If I can make characters relatable, then I can use story and style to keep readers turning the page.

To improve my storytelling skills, I must keep consuming stories. I must consume popular and off-the-beaten-path content. I must seek out stories that I wouldn't normally read. This will help me build my muscle.

To improve my style, I must also study the masters, but I must decide what I want my calling cards to be. This is a work in progress.

. . .

Productivity

The next essential skill for a master to have is productivity. Productivity is often overlooked and underrated. However, let me ask you this: if you could be a mega-best-selling author with two books that sell millions or hundreds of books that sell hundreds of millions, which would you pick? I think we know the answer.

The "prolific" author is a stigma and an enigma. Readers and writers alike have been conditioned to look down upon this type of writer, dismissing them as hacks who only write mediocre stories for profit. But, as I have said many times throughout this series, that's bullshit. I consider myself to be a neo pulp writer, and if some readers don't like that, they aren't in my target audience anyway.

Productivity is creativity. The more productive one is and the more effective and efficient they are at telling good stories quickly, the better their stories will be. Now, is it possible that there is a limit to how productive one can be before the quality of their stories begins to suffer? Yes, I admit that. It is possible to write so quickly that quality control goes out the window. I don't advocate that, and I never have.

Everyone must find their optimal writing speed; additionally, they must find the speed where their quality breaks apart so they know their limits. But limits can be extended. They are just indicators at a point in time and must be continuously tested against one's skill level and knowledge. Otherwise, stagnation sets in.

A master writer can create book after book on a reliable and consistent schedule so that readers always know what to expect and when to expect it. This master stays top of mind for their readers, which is the best (and least talked about) method of making money. It just works.

The moral of the story: write fast, write well, and release as quickly as possible.

Yet, I have failed miserably in this area. I write quickly, but I don't publish on a consistent schedule. This is something I've always wanted to improve, but I have struggled, given that I have a young family and a full-time job. I have so many competing priorities for my attention that I have not made progress in this area. If I am to become a master, this *must* become one of my key strengths.

Now that I am sitting on a portfolio that will soon be greater than one hundred books, the *number* of books I have published isn't terribly important. Readers' eyes bug out of their heads just the same when they hear that you have 100 books versus 300 books. Their eyes bug out just a little more when you get into the upper hundreds, but then you have bigger problems to deal with—namely that they will be overwhelmed and intimidated by such a gargantuan portfolio.

As I have written in previous volumes of this series, another critical skill of a master is the ability to get the right reader to the right book at the right time.

The estate of Barbara Cartland does this better than any other author I have ever seen. With a portfolio of over 700 books, the average Barbara Cartland reader has no idea where to start at the outset of their journey with her. Fortunately, Cartland's website takes care of this and recommends the best starting points. This is also why I have developed my Book Wizard tool. The goal is the same.

As my portfolio grows, I want to make it easy to get the right book in front of the right reader at the right time. It's much easier to do this now than it will be when I have several hundred books under my name. Better to start with a solution and evolve it over time than to address it down the road when it is too late. I believe that you can manage the reader intimidation and overwhelm that comes with a large portfolio if you do it early.

While I have made strides in this area as well, I am not quite where I want to be yet.

Massive productivity also has other benefits. It means you can take advantage of opportunities as they arise. If an editor needs a short story for an anthology based on a certain subject matter, you can instantly write something that meets their specs with a high level of writing quality, therefore increasing your earning potential and ability to get in front of more readers. If an organizer reaches out about a speaking opportunity, a master can develop a talk that meets the organizer's needs and blows the audience away.

Why do I care so much about public speaking? The masters are asked to speak all the time. They're in constant demand on the speaking circuit, at expositions, conferences, seminars, podcasts, and video interviews. I would bet my house that masters like Dean Koontz and Nora Roberts get so many speaking engagements that they could travel anywhere in the world whenever they wanted. Granted, I would also bet that they turn down the majority of speaking requests they receive, but the point stands.

Speaking is very, very lucrative. Masters probably don't like to speak that much because it takes them away from writing, but remember what I just said about productivity. What if it were true that you could travel a substantial part of the year *and* still produce more books than 99 percent of writers?

This would require some simple math. The master would need to determine how many books they write per year *without* traveling. Next, they would need to calculate the average number of words they write per day and the average number of days they would be away on a trip. Finally, they would need to do some quick math to determine what percentage of a novel a trip would cost them.

For most writers who enter the speaking circuit, the following predictable process occurs:

1. The author desires to get into the speaking circuit and will speak everywhere they can.
2. The author overextends themselves on the speaking circuit, burning out and not desiring to speak anymore because of the loss of productivity. Perhaps their book output diminishes or they just don't feel joy in speaking anymore.
3. The author cuts back on their speaking and focuses on their writing.

This pattern is predictable and is ultimately the right decision for many, but there is another way.

If the author could learn to write reliably while on the road as I have using tools like dictation, then the author could write anywhere. It wouldn't matter where they were; it would only matter how many words they could write while on the road. Naturally, this number would probably be lower than what they would achieve if they were in their normal writing environment, but progress is progress.

Let's say that they could write 50 percent of the words they normally do. That changes the math dramatically. It allows the author to maximize their time on the speaking circuit while remaining insanely productive.

Speaking is not only lucrative because of the high-dollar speaker fees that the masters can command; it is also the perfect forum for retail author marketing. Think about it: how else would one meet their fans directly?

When one becomes a master, they have the opportunity to pour gasoline on word-of-mouth sales. Readers remember things like authors staying at a book signing until every reader has their book signed. They remember authors who listen to them, thank them for being readers, and offer words of encouragement about whatever problem they're dealing with. They remember charming speeches. They remember a speaker who shows up on time and who arrives with gifts or special items that the public would not otherwise get. My point is that this is such an underrated part of being a master in the 21st century that it is something I intend to take full advantage of if I am ever in the position to do so.

People Skills

The final skill that a master must cultivate is superior people skills. This may seem like a strange thing for a writer to develop. After all, we pride ourselves on being introverts, and we make our living sitting in a dark room by ourselves and making things up. However, a master works with people from all walks of life: editors, cover designers, accountants, lawyers, consultants, publishers, readers from all over, and so on. They must be adept at talking to anyone in this wide spectrum at any time. Because they have accumulated substantial wealth (or have the potential to) and because their name carries impressive notoriety, they must be careful about whom they associate with, whom they lend their names to, and who manages certain elements of their business. Thieves, crooks, and scammers will abound, and they must be as good judges of character as possible, knowing that there will inevitably be mistakes.

Having superior people skills can help the master navigate this perilous landscape. They must understand body language, anticipate a person's next move correctly, and guard themselves, their families, and their work at all costs. This is not for the faint of heart and requires a certain personality type. The personality type of which I speak is one who can be creative in one moment and iron-fisted in the next.

If I sound cynical, it is only because of horror stories I've read and anecdotes I've heard about the lives of mega best-sellers. That's all I'll say about the "cynical" part of people skills.

There is a practical side to this as well. A master must work with many types of people, so they must learn how to be a team player and how to manage people to get what they want as efficiently as possible. The master must motivate everyone around him to do their best work and service of the readers. They must also motivate readers to spread the word about their books. This requires a certain type of charisma that not all authors have.

Romance authors excel in this area more than any other type of author I know. It helps that they have a motivated fan base, but romance authors are some of the most charismatic authors you will meet—especially the masters.

In any case, a wide and deep toolbox of people skills is required to become a master—at least one who has a long and successful career.

Bringing It All Together

A master must develop superior writing, productivity, and people skills. If I want to be a master, these are the skills I must focus on.

For writing skills, I must improve my character and story skills. I must also develop a trademark style.

For productivity, I must continue being productive and

finding new ways to be more effective and efficient in my writing life. I must also improve the consistency with which I publish books.

For people skills, I must continue to engage with a broad spectrum of people in my job as a corporate executive and apply those lessons to the writing world, particularly lessons in law and business.

When you take all of these skills together, you have a recipe for a master in the making.

I desire very much to achieve this level, but I know it will be hard work. Nothing easy is worth doing, right?

MEDITATIONS ON MINDFULNESS

The first stop in my mindset journey was a meditation on mindfulness.

"Mindfulness" is a trendy new thing these days, with many companies and organizations pushing the benefits of being mindful.

I've had issues with the mindfulness movement over the years. My biggest problem with it is that it has become a corporate buzzword. Employers want you to be mindful so that you can be more productive. When an employer encourages employees to be more mindful, it often means that the employer has created a working environment so miserable that its employees have lost themselves. It is impossible to be mindful in such an environment. If you do become mindful, you do so to serve the interests of your employer, not yourself, your health, or your family. Sorry, just keeping it real.

Mindfulness must be a choice, and that choice must be made by the individual because they need it, not because someone is simply telling them to be more mindful. I suppose this is why I've always subconsciously written off the term.

Anyway, I experienced a mindset shift on mindfulness by

accident. I happened to watch a three-hour video compilation of Michael Singer. Singer is an author and spiritual coach who teaches the benefits of mindfulness, and for the first time, someone finally convinced me why it is important. *Of course* we need to be mindful in our lives, but how do we do that? What does it feel like? How do I know if I'm doing it correctly?

I want to be mindful to be more effective in my life overall, not just at the workplace. Besides, there is nothing employer wellness programs can teach me anyway. (If I sound cynical, it's because I've fallen for these types of programs in the past and gotten nothing from them.)

I learned a lot from Michael Singer. I will summarize some of the most important learnings.

The Moment in Front of You

I don't know if Singer invented this saying, but he says it a lot: "The moment in front of you is not bothering you. You are bothering yourself about the moment in front of you." In other words, whenever we are experiencing stress, the problem itself is not the issue. The problem is our minds. The problem is anxiety.

This is familiar ground for me because I teach about anxiety all the time. In my book *The Pocket Guide to Pantsing*, I talk about anxiety and how it is such an impediment to writers during the manuscript drafting process. It's funny how we can learn things again, but in a different way and on a deeper level.

Anxiety is so deep-seated and ubiquitous in our lives that we don't always notice it. We may notice it when we are writing a book, but it presents itself differently at work, for example.

Therefore, learning to identify anxiety in all of its different forms is an incredible benefit.

One way to identify anxiety is by understanding what it truly is. Most people would tell you that they are not anxious people, yet their lives are filled with anxiety. This is because people have been conditioned to believe that anxiety is like what they see on television—a sweaty, nervous person on the verge of having a breakdown while chewing on a pencil or pacing on a rug. But anxiety is more subtle than that.

Singer's message is that mindfulness is simply learning to be aware of the moments you're in. Every moment that happens around the world is just a moment. The world belongs to itself and there's very little you can do to change it most of the time. Even if you feel anxiety about something, it won't matter to others, so the key is not to not feel anxious; it's to recognize your anxiety and release it.

Recognize and release.

When someone cuts you off on the highway, it doesn't matter how you feel about it. No matter what you say or do, the person won't care. So recognize the anger you feel, acknowledge it and why you feel that way, and then release it.

So as Singer says, "The moment in front of you is not bothering you. You are bothering yourself about the moment in front of you." This is also true of moments behind you.

Don't Learn How to Open; Learn How to Avoid Closing

The natural reaction when we experience stress is to close ourselves off and avoid it. This is a protective mechanism.

Yet, whenever someone says something mean or does something that bothers us, it still bothers us even if we close ourselves off. In fact, we close and wrestle with the problem, and the other person never even knows it.

Singer's message is to avoid closing. It's not healthy to keep these emotions inside of us. It's far better to release them. He argues that whenever we encounter something messy in life, we should see it as an opportunity to improve ourselves. When your spouse pushes your buttons, address the problem. When a coworker tries to sabotage you at work, call them out on it. While it may create short-term discomfort, the problem will no longer dwell inside you. You may not always get this right, but you're choosing to live by a code that respects yourself and your own mental health. It also respects others because it allows you to have deeper relationships with them by confronting interpersonal conflicts head-on.

Singer advises to clean the inside of our spirits so that we release as many of these problems as possible. The cleaner we are, the better.

The question isn't "How do I open myself?" The answer is "How do I not close?" Singer argues that adopting this mindset shift will cause a massive change in your life.

Ignore the Personal Voice in Your Head

Singer rails against the critical voice. He doesn't call it that, but he calls it the "inner voice" that dictates your feelings. It's the voice that tells you, "I like that person." Or, "I don't like that person." Or, "if it rains tomorrow, I'll be miserable because I am supposed to host a picnic." Or, "if I could only buy that BMW, I'll be happy."

Singer decided to take an entire year to listen and observe

this voice. He didn't understand it because there was no rhyme or reason to why it recommended the things it did. What he learned: the voice is crazy when it comes to personal affairs. Absolutely crazy. It changes its mind all the time, it leads us down wrong paths, and it causes so much trouble in our lives. (Note: he believes that the mind does not do this in other areas of our lives—just the personal.)

Singer concluded that he didn't want to listen to that voice. He instead decided to surrender himself to life. If he decided to do something, it wouldn't be because the voice told him to. If he decided he didn't like someone, it wouldn't be because the voice told him. Instead, he would seek the facts and draw his own conclusions.

As the Greeks say, "Your senses will fool you." So will your mind.

Singer's conclusions about not listening to the critical voice can be applied to any writing career. It can also be applied to one's personal life in general.

Bringing the Lessons Together

So what can I apply from Michael Singer? There are so many lessons.

First, his talks are a reminder not to get stuck in the theater of my mind. By focusing on the moment ahead of me, recognizing the anxiety I may feel and then releasing it, I can meet the moment better. This applies when I'm in the middle of a story and don't know what's going to happen next, or if I'm worried about an important meeting at work.

Second, I can do a better job of recognizing those "closing" moments when I would normally close myself off. Instead of closing, I can stay open and meet the moment head-on, even if it sucks. Even if I don't necessarily have the interpersonal skills to handle that moment with finesse, it will serve me better in the long run. This is true in all areas of my life, but especially my personal life.

Finally, I must keep ignoring that damn voice in my head. The critical voice wants nothing more than you being stuck in its endless loop of fear and gloom. With soon to be over 100 books to my name, I'd say I'm a master at kicking the critical voice's ass, but I must remember to stay vigilant. The further you progress in your life, the more the critical voice evolves new tools to try to stop you. It's like Wile E. Coyote, always coming up with some new cockamamie idea to kill the roadrunner. Fortunately, Wile E. Coyote always ends up with a rocket in his face and plummeting into a canyon below while the roadrunner meeps and dashes down the road with a smile on its face. That's a lesson we can all learn from: be the roadrunner (just don't run away from your problems).

I'm grateful for the talks I discovered by Michael Singer, and I look forward to learning more from him in the future.

WRITING AFTER A BREAK

I took another break from writing this quarter to deal with some residual health issues from earlier in the year. It was nothing serious, but I finally made a commitment to eat a healthy, nutritious diet and get more than the recommended amount of exercise. This required my full time and mental energy so that I could make better decisions and learn how to make them unconsciously.

The break was only a few weeks, so it wasn't hard to get back into writing. I want to share some of the lessons I learned.

It seems to me that every break I take is different in its own way. My last break was facilitated by a serious health issue that prevented me from writing; this break was facilitated by me being proactive. I *could have* written during this period, but I chose not to. During the break, I remained minimally productive, keeping my email inbox at or near zero, staying up-to-date on my to-dos and following up on projects in the works with others. I kept all of my calendar appointments and, with the exception of no writing, everything was business as usual.

That made it easier to sit down at the keyboard again—much, much easier.

I still had some struggles, however. I identified a weakness in my current productivity workflow. Here is my current workflow:

- Day A: Maintenance Days where I focus on handling emails and loose ends. I let the demands of the day be my primary concern.
- Day B: Action Item Days where I focus exclusively on my to-dos. I work on projects and (mostly) ignore my email and other loose ends.

This productivity workflow allows me to make progress toward my projects while also maintaining the business. It prevents me from falling behind on projects and then spending several days catching up. It also prevents me from falling behind on business maintenance items and email.

However, this workflow had one obvious blind spot that I kicked myself for not seeing: I don't include writing in my to-do list. Writing is just something that I do every day. I don't set goals; I just write and see where I end up. My action items are reserved for non-writing tasks I must do to maintain the business or move it forward. The entire reason I created this workflow was because I focused *too much* on my writing and not on other areas of the business.

The revelation? I need a writing day, one day in the workflow where I *only* focus on writing new words.

Therefore, the new workflow would be:

- Maintenance Day
- Action Item Day
- Writing Day

This workflow would allow me to maximize my progress in

maintaining the business, working on important projects such as portfolio management and joint marketing efforts with other authors, *and* doing the most important thing that any writer can do: write more words as feverishly as possible.

Of course, I still write every day on my maintenance and project days; I just write *more* on my writing days.

Productivity workflows only work for a season, and I know that many volumes from now, I will probably have to change my workflow again due to whatever circumstances happen in my life at that time, but this workflow is working very well for me right now, and I'm going to take advantage of it every opportunity I can.

SHORT STORY ERRORS

In previous volumes, I discussed my adventures in writing short stories and submitting them to magazines. This quarter marks the one-year anniversary of starting that project. It also marks the end of the submission process for several stories because they have made their rounds through all of the professional (paying) magazines.

Unfortunately, major markets rejected every story I wrote. Therefore, it is time to create a short story series with those stories that were rejected so that I can monetize them and utilize these pieces of intellectual property. I don't like short stories sitting around, so I need to put them to work as quickly as possible once submission markets reject them.

However, there was one aspect in this project that I failed to consider: anthology submissions. I received news of a short story anthology where the editor was looking for a specific type of story that matched one of the ones that I had written. I submitted the story to the editor and didn't think anything of it.

A few months later, I discovered another anthology also looking for submissions. Without realizing it, I submitted that same story to the second anthology. Only by accident did I discover my mistake, which mortified me. I go out of my way *not* to do simultaneous submissions, though I wish more magazines allowed them.

As mortified as I was, I decided that the best way to handle this situation was to do nothing temporarily. It was possible that both editors could reject my work, in which case I would be worried for nothing. I would only take action if one editor accepted the story.

Editor A promised to make a decision within one month. Editor B wasn't even going to start reading the slush pile for four months, so I took a calculated gamble and made a plan.

This is the plan: if either editor accepts the story, I will immediately email the other editor and withdraw the story from that anthology, hope for the best, and pray I don't burn a bridge. Regardless of what happens, it is a valuable (and hard) lesson learned.

Did the plan work? Stay tuned to the next volume to find out if this story ends in success or disaster. I'm sitting on pins and needles, myself...

Anyway, there was a lesson here. I track my submissions on a Microsoft Excel sheet in my master publishing file. For each story, I track which major market I've submitted to so I always know where a story is. The point is to (obviously) avoid simultaneous submissions. However, I did not track my submission to anthologies. I didn't consider them when I built the spreadsheet. I easily rectified this by adding a couple of extra columns to the spreadsheet. I will now only submit a story to an anthology *after* it has cleared the major markets.

Now that I also track anthology submissions, I should be able to avoid simultaneous submission disasters in the future.

LESSONS IN VOCABULARY FROM DEAN KOONTZ

I study Dean Koontz a lot. He's one of the best practitioners of the writing craft still living today. More so than other masters, his command of the English language is Shakespearean in that he uses words and phrases that are intensely evocative. Yet, you don't need a dictionary to enjoy him. I've yet to read a writer who writes like him, though there are many who use beautiful language. But there is only one Dean Koontz.

I used his novel *Odd Thomas* to do a quick study. I wanted to find out how many unique words he uses in the first 25 percent of the novel. I could then extrapolate that to get a sense of how many he might use in the full novel. I felt this exercise would give me a good idea of how frequently I should be stretching my vocabulary. I also felt it might give me some hints on how to find those words that Koontz uses.

The first chapter of *Odd Thomas* is approximately 3,800 words. In it, Koontz used 33 interesting words and phrases, which is 1 unique instance every 115 words.

If this held true for the entire 39-chapter novel (103,000 words), that would result in approximately 895 unique words per novel, or somewhere between 8 and 9 unique words for every 1,000 words. Wow, that's a lot of work.

For Dean, this is a skill that comes naturally to him, like breathing. It likely took him many years to make this skill subconscious. However, if I want to acquire this skill for myself, I must practice it.

Now that I had a rough approximation of how frequently I needed to use interesting words (without going overboard or being silly about it), I now knew how to practice.

In previous volumes of the series, I've discussed at length the importance of using the five senses *at least* every 500 words. It's the technique that Dean Wesley Smith taught me, and it's the technique that every master uses.

In thinking about this, I arrived at an interesting thought: how many of the unique and interesting words that Koontz uses are *sensory*— in other words, how frequently is he doing double duty? Obviously, the best time to use an evocative word is when you are pairing it with a sense, but not always. For fun, I guessed that Koontz paired his evocative words with sensory details at least 33 percent of the time. When I went back to the text to test my hypothesis, I was exactly right. Koontz pairs his evocative words with sensory details approximately 33 percent of the time. To be sure, I checked a few chapters, and I observed a variance of between 30 and 40 percent.

Here's what all of this means and why it is so important.

If Koontz is using 8 evocative words out of 1,000, then that means that, in a 500-word section, he is using 4 unique words per 500 words. This means that in the opening of a chapter, every time I use a sense, I should use something *more* evocative than I normally would (but that doesn't hamper my style or make the reader reach for a dictionary—remember, this is Koontz's trademark). Then, I need to use three *more* evocative words or phrases that can be sensory or not sensory. The three extra evocative words are the delta that will make the difference. I'm already doing this to some degree, but I need to be more intentional about it.

And that's just the beginning. The numbers I cited were just averages. I would be willing to bet that Koontz uses *more* evocative words in high stakes, high emotion scenes, and fewer in slower paced scenes. This technique is intricately tied to every other craft element: pacing, character development, dialogue, and more. It's a tool that can work for you in all seasons no matter what you are writing. That's why I believe it is such a valuable skill to develop.

If I start practicing this skill today, sure, I'll see a few benefits here and there, but it's unlikely to improve my book sales right away. The real value in mastering a skill like this is the benefit when I write a best-selling book at some point in the future. Imagine I write a book that hits it big in three years after practicing the skill every day. Maybe by that point, I will have made the skill unconscious and blended it with my style so that I have truly leveled up my writing. That will keep readers engaged, therefore increasing my sales and my readership.

I know, vocabulary isn't sexy. It's also not something that many self-published writers think about much. When we think of vocabulary, we think of stodgy literary writers in ivory towers writing purple prose, and we forget the true power that words have when a writer pairs skill with imagination without talking down to the reader. When that occurs, the result is nothing short of magic.

I look forward to practicing the skill in the future. One day, if I'm successful, it would be the greatest compliment if readers say the same thing about me that they say about Koontz. Honestly, if I can consciously develop this skill to be even a fraction as good as him, I've won.

BECOME A TECHNOLOGY
AND DATA-DRIVEN WRITER

REVISITING MY EXPENSES

It has been a while since I have done a deep dive into my expenses. I keep track of my expenses every month, but I haven't done a thorough analysis on how they have changed over time.

I discovered—like many business owners do—that I had some room for improvement.

For example, I was paying for several website hosting add-ons that I didn't need. I also had some subscriptions that were no longer necessary.

On a spreadsheet, I did the following analysis:

- I recorded each expense and how much I paid for it monthly and annually. For expenses that I pay biennially, I calculated how much it cost me annually.
- I recorded what I paid for the expense in each of the last three years.
- I did a yearly calculation of how much (or less) the expense increased year over year.

This exercise is always eye-opening because it confirms many of the things you know to be true about your expenses but also smacks you in the face with things you don't expect. For example, when I sorted the spreadsheet monthly expenses from most expensive to least expensive, I discovered exactly how much each of my expenses were truly costing me each month. This is important because I pay for many of my expenses annually and biennially, so it's easy to lose track of what they actually cost me.

This exercise also led me to ask the question, "What expenses are truly needed?"

I find that expenses fall into one of three categories:

1. You can justify them because they bring in more revenue than the expense. An example is your website hosting.
2. You can't justify the expense because the cost is more than any revenue you could ever hope to bring in.
3. The expense can't be justified with revenue, but it is so essential to the business that if you didn't have it, you would lose a significant amount of time or money.

I went through the spreadsheet and looked for opportunities to cut and reduce expenses without any material impact to the business. For example, I was paying for the Adobe Creative Cloud subscription for Adobe apps, but I don't really use them. I mostly use Photoshop. I purchased the premium subscription plan with aspirations to use InDesign, Audition, and Premiere, but that didn't materialize. Therefore, I reduced my subscription to Photoshop only and cut my expenses from $600 per year to $200 with no impact to the business.

This sounds silly, but this sort of thing happens all the time when you run a business. The key is to develop discipline so that it happens less often.

The spreadsheet also illuminated opportunities in my business that I'm not taking advantage of. For example, one of my higher monthly expenses is Teachable, an online service where I host my courses. I signed up for the service this year, but my plans to promote my courses didn't materialize. If I want to keep using it, I need to do a better job of driving people to my courses to justify the expense.

Overall, despite the opportunities, my expenses are in a much better position than they were in previous years. I truly believe that I have as lean of a writing business now as I can have. My expenses are optimized, I'm not leaving money on the table, and I have a good plan for increasing my revenue mix.

That's the value of doing a deep dive into your expenses every now and again.

TRANSITIONING CLOUD STORAGE
PROVIDERS

In the previous chapter, I discussed a deep dive of my expenses. I uncovered an opportunity to revisit my cloud storage plans. For various reasons, I had plans with Google Drive, Apple iCloud, and Microsoft One Drive.

For Apple, having extra storage on my iCloud account makes sense because I have a lot of photos and documents that I frequently share between my phone and laptop. The paltry storage limits they give you on the free plan just don't cut it for me, so I have no problem paying one dollar per month for additional storage. This decision made sense a few years ago, and it still makes sense now.

For Microsoft, it makes zero sense to have Word, Excel, and PowerPoint as my primary productivity apps without taking advantage of Microsoft One Drive's autosave capabilities. In fact, not doing so is playing with fire. I want the benefit of autosave with every document I work on without having to think about it, so having a storage plan makes a great deal of sense, especially because (at the time of this writing) you don't have to pay extra for storage because the Microsoft 365 subscription plan includes up to one TB of storage.

Given that Word, Excel, and PowerPoint are my productivity apps of choice, it makes the most sense that OneDrive would be my primary cloud storage app, right?

Wrong.

For the past decade, Google Drive has been my primary cloud storage solution. I've always had good luck with Drive and it served me well. But when I looked at Drive under a microscope, I realized that my business needs have changed. In 2014, when I committed to Google Drive, I had a completely different business. Scrivener was my primary writing app. I didn't know one end of a spreadsheet from another. I wouldn't have touched Microsoft Word with a ten-foot pole. The term "AI" wasn't even in most writers' vocabularies. OneDrive and iCloud weren't nearly as powerful as they are today. Google (and Dropbox to a lesser extent) were the de facto leaders in the cloud storage space. Therefore, it made sense to purchase storage plans through Google Drive.

But for the reasons I listed above, Drive no longer makes sense in any capacity for me in 2023. Therefore, I took the following actions:

- I canceled my Drive storage plan, migrating exclusively to OneDrive, with my iCloud plan in place as needed for saving photos and sending files between my Apple devices.
- I deleted all of the documents on my Drive account, thinking that I no longer needed them.
- I saved myself $130 per year.

The decision was the right one, but there an unintended consequence. I forgot that the reader bonuses in several of my books were hosted on Google Drive. I began receiving emails from readers letting me know that the resources I provided in the back of my books were no longer available. I quickly discovered my error and worked feverishly to correct it. It taught me a valuable lesson.

I learned a few things about Google Drive that, if I had known before signing up, I would have done quite a few things differently.

First, Google Sheets is an amazingly convenient and free alternative to Microsoft Excel that has most of the functionality one would need in Excel. However, there is a poison pill if you *create* a Google Sheet: it can only be viewed online. When you back up the sheet, you don't actually back it up. You back up a *shortcut* to the sheet on Google's servers. Therefore, when you delete your data from Google, you also delete the spreadsheet with no possibility of recovering it. When I discovered that a few of my Google Sheets were deleted, I immediately logged into Backblaze, my backup software that I use in emergencies to recover lost data. Backblaze didn't help me one iota because it only backed up the shortcut to the spreadsheet, which ceremoniously went nowhere.

Yikes...

Another thing I learned is that Google allows you to restore files you've deleted as long as you do so within 30 days. I was able to retrieve all my files with no problem, but the retrieval process reset all of the permissions on files I deleted. Files that I had shared with others or made public (to be used in the back of my books) were reset to private. Even though I had the files restored, readers still couldn't access them.

Double yikes...

I suppose Google does all of these things to keep users locked into its ecosystem.

Now that I transitioned to Microsoft OneDrive, I didn't want to make that same mistake again. I don't know why I didn't host the files I wanted to share directly on my WordPress website. That would have been the best option. You live and you learn.

Fortunately, I kept a record of all the books that had bonuses in the back matter noted in my master publishing file. With just a couple of clicks, I got the list, uploaded the bonuses to my WordPress site, redirected the links, and breathed a sigh of relief. Then, I deleted all of my Google Drive files again permanently.

Once I migrated to OneDrive, I canceled my Google One stored subscription plan and rested easy knowing that I wouldn't have to do this again for a very long time, if ever.

One day, I discovered by accident that Backblaze wasn't backing up my OneDrive files. This was strange, because Backblaze is supposed to back up everything on your computer on a regular basis. It turned out that Backblaze hadn't backed up a single OneDrive file in the entire month after my transition.

I learned that Microsoft stores its files in an odd manner. I don't fully understand the technical reasons why, but to oversimplify it, when you save a file on your computer and tell your computer to back it up into the cloud, Apple iCloud, Google Drive, and Dropbox all save the copy of the file on your computer *first* before uploading it into the cloud. This makes sense and is how I would expect cloud storage programs to work. However, Microsoft saves its files into the cloud first and *then* downloads them onto your computer.

Let me give you an example of why this doesn't make any sense. Let's say I'm working on a Microsoft Word document. When I'm done, I save a copy onto OneDrive. I need to send the document to someone, so I open Microsoft Outlook, compose the email, and click the attach button. You would think that the file would be on my computer, right? No, it is not, because it is in the cloud, and I have to wait for OneDrive to download it to my computer first, a process that can take anywhere from five to ten minutes.

I would love for someone at Microsoft to explain to me why this is a good idea. When you create a file on your computer, you should have immediate access to it. But I digress.

This peculiar technical decision by the Microsoft OneDrive team is compounded by the fact that when Microsoft OneDrive files reside on your computer, they don't actually reside on your computer. Sure, you can access them, edit them, delete them, and do whatever you want, but Backblaze cannot read them. Backblaze doesn't even know they're there.

I checked Backblaze's support forums, where other users lamented over this problem as well. Some of them had lost significant amounts of data before discovering the issue. The Backblaze team attempted to solve this problem but gave up in June 2023, when they officially announced that the program would no longer support Microsoft OneDrive backups.

Great. I wish I had known this before migrating to Microsoft OneDrive! Shame on me for not considering that angle, but the silver lining was that I hadn't lost any data at this point. It was a happy accident that I discovered this in the first place.

At this point, I had a decision to make. I had just broken up with Google, who didn't take kindly to me doing so. I wasn't about to go back to Google Drive when I didn't use their services on a regular basis. I'm not enmeshed in the Google ecosystem, so the decision to leave Drive was the right one. But I couldn't stay with OneDrive. I was risking serious data loss if I did.

The remaining solutions? Dropbox or Box, but I wasn't really a fan of either of them. There was also Apple iCloud, which made more sense given that I am firmly entrenched in the

Apple ecosystem, so making a move there would make sense. Also, Backblaze had no problem backing up iCloud files—I confirmed that and tested it for myself.

So, iCloud it was. Fortunately, the transition from Microsoft OneDrive to Apple iCloud wasn't nearly as challenging as the transition from Drive to Microsoft OneDrive. This is because I made all my mistakes when transferring from Google to Microsoft. All I had to do was transfer the files now.

I only had one more serious and inconvenient decision to make. The reason I wanted to transition to Microsoft OneDrive was because of the autosave feature while using Microsoft Office applications. There's comfort in knowing that when you create a Word, Excel, or PowerPoint file, it is automatically being backed up in the cloud without you having to worry about it. Also, I can't prove this, but I really feel that Microsoft Office applications just work better and smoother in OneDrive.

So, I had to choose:

- Did I forgo the autosave feature altogether, or,
- Did I transfer all of my non-Microsoft Office files to iCloud while keeping Microsoft Office files in OneDrive so I could get the best of both worlds?

At the time of this writing, I chose to migrate 99 percent of my files to Apple iCloud while keeping certain Microsoft Office files in OneDrive. I don't like this solution, but it's the best thing I could come up with right now until and unless Microsoft gets their act together.

And thus concludes my crazy journey across many different cloud storage providers. I learned a lot, and I'm grateful for the experience, but it would be nice if I never had to think about this again.

These are the sorts of things that pop up when you have

been in business a long time and have as many books and resources as I do. Hopefully, you didn't find this chapter tedious, and perhaps it will help you avoid the same pitfalls in the future.

BUILDING A CONTINGENCY PLAN

In a previous volume of this series, I wrote about my adventures with GeniusLink. GeniusLink is a link redirection service that allows you to redirect traffic to any site of your choosing based on numerous criteria. The service offers many features that I have found invaluable in my marketing, and I have no intention of terminating the service anytime soon.

However, using a service like GeniusLink introduces a vulnerability in my business. Your links become invalid the moment you terminate your subscription.

This is dangerous for many reasons:

- When you die, it's possible your heirs could cancel the service without understanding why it is important.
- The company could be acquired or merged with another company.
- The company could go out of business.
- The company could raise its rates to something unaffordable.
- And so on.

As I said, I have no concerns with GeniusLink or its financial stability. I'm just looking out for my business and my readers.

What if something happened that put my GeniusLinks in danger? It doesn't matter what; all that matters is any scenario could happen that could invalidate my links.

What would I do if such an event happened? What would the cost be if I did nothing? What would the cost be to implement a solution? These are questions I asked myself, and hours later, I had a winning strategy just in case such a scenario were to occur.

The Plan

First, I needed to figure out how many GeniusLinks I was using, and *where* I was using them. This was the hardest part.

I use GeniusLinks in the following places:

1. the book pages on my website where I link to Amazon
2. the descriptions of my YouTube videos
3. the descriptions of my podcast "The Writer's Journey"

I felt pretty good about this inventory.

Next, I needed a way to identify *where* the GeniusLinks were. For my website, that's easy--every book page has one.

For YouTube, I purchased a tool called TubeBuddy that allowed me to perform a find and replace across the video descriptions of my three hundred-plus videos. By searching for the unique string of characters at the beginning of every

GeniusLink, I identified every link in less than five minutes. On a Microsoft Excel spreadsheet, I listed the name of the YouTube video, a link to the video, the GeniusLink, and a description of the link for future reference.

For my podcast, I simply copied the XML from the RSS feed and pasted that into Microsoft Word. The RSS feed is public-facing and contains the metadata for a podcast, including show notes! In less than five minutes, I identified the Genius-Links in production in my podcast, and I notated them on another tab in the Microsoft Excel spreadsheet.

This entire exercise took approximately one hour. It gave me a working list of precisely what I needed to address in the event of a crisis. I estimated that it would take approximately two hours to fix these links if something were to happen to GeniusLink. I also included the replacement link for future reference to make my life easier.

This was an easy exercise and it will save me a ton of money someday. There is nothing worse than a reader loving your content, clicking your video or podcast, and finding a broken link.

That's the power of contingency plans. They help you in situations like this. While no plan is perfect, I am proud to have one in place.

THE ADVENT OF THE MICROSOFT COPILOTS

Earlier this year, Microsoft disrupted the internet browser industry with the introduction of its new Bing Copilot, an AI assistant powered by ChatGPT designed to help answer questions and make browsing the web easier. Bing Copilot also helps users do creative tasks such as writing emails, developing recipes, and even generating AI art. At the time, I believed it would truly be a disruptive technology, but *only* if Microsoft didn't follow the same route as Amazon and other tech giants. You see, Amazon Alexa was also a disruptive technology, but Amazon stopped developing it. Alexa is nothing more than a glorified smartphone assistant that doesn't understand you half the time. Siri was also amazingly disruptive when it came out, but Apple also stopped improving it. Until I see otherwise, I have no reason to believe that Microsoft won't make the same mistake. This is what monopolistic corporations do. However, there is some hope.

In September 2023, Microsoft unveiled another copilot: Windows 11 Copilot. Similar to Bing Copilot, Windows 11 Copilot helps users navigate Windows 11 more easily. Early reports of the copilot are mixed at best, but the application has promise.

Far more interesting to me, however, is the upcoming Microsoft Office 365 Copilot. This new brand of copilots is designed to help people maximize their creativity in Power-Point. It can create slides, proofread text, and even suggest additional content on slides.

In Excel, it can create graphs based on the data in a spreadsheet and analyze that data for the user, making the active data analysis much simpler and open to non-data geeks.

Microsoft Word is the real copilot to watch. It can write and design documents, summarize long strings of text, and—most importantly—edit text. I haven't been able to confirm that this functionality exists, but I have seen the possibility and screenshots. There is in fact an Edit button. If this can do what I think it can do, it will be a game changer for writers everywhere.

Think about: Microsoft's Editor tool sucks. It barely understands the laws of English, and the recommendations it makes are head-scratching at best. If you're lucky, it will help you catch a handful of typos in a full-length manuscript. By comparison, tools like Grammarly and ProWritingAid will help you catch dozens of errors, and that's being conservative.

If Microsoft Word can help writers produce cleaner manuscripts, that will be a seismic change. So many writers focus on Scrivener and other writing apps designed to make the writing process easier, and for good reason. But, one of the problems with the current writing app landscape is that it doesn't allow for a smooth migration of data. I've said this many times, but it is a serious problem that writers must write their books in their writing app of choice, export it to Microsoft Word, send it to the editor, who edits the book in Word, receive the edited manuscript back, and then transport it to yet *another* app for e-book and paperback formatting. It's a mess, and it's one of the primary reasons I switched back to Microsoft Word. I use it for macros, and my editor is going to require a Word file anyway, so why not just use Word?

Anyway, I've litigated this issue enough that I don't need to go into it any further.

There will likely be other use cases with the Microsoft Word copilot that I haven't considered, and that's exciting. It's possible that writers are going to get a level-up on their ability to create cleaner manuscripts, and I think that's great.

I'm cynical, but I sincerely hope that I am wrong.

These copilots are amazing technologies that have the ability to completely change how we work. If Microsoft is true to their word and embrace the promise of this technology that they have capitalized on, then nothing will ever be the same. I don't like hyperbole, but it is warranted here. It's not difficult to imagine a near future where creating a PowerPoint slide deck is a thing of the past. Just have the AI do it. Don't like spreadsheets? No problem; let the AI handle it and just check its work. Have to put together a brochure at the last minute? Let the AI do it. This technology promises to remove much of the creative grunt work we have to do every day. For that reason, it will certainly eliminate jobs, and that's a tragedy. However, it is also true that it may create new opportunities. Rather than focus on the negativity, I prefer to focus on the possibilities, which are endless.

The Microsoft Office 365 Copilot is slated to launch for enterprise customers in the fourth quarter of 2023. I expect it to launch for personal customers sometime around the middle of 2024. And when it does, I will be the first in line to try out the new copilot for Word.

I strongly recommend that people don't sleep on these copilots. Even though it's highly possible that they won't be all they're cracked up to be, it's also possible that they could be game changers.

THE STATE OF AI ART GENERATORS

AI art continues its meteoric climb. More services launched and/or rose to prominence this year, and they have competed to gain market share. At the time of this writing, the biggest players are Stable Diffusion, MidJourney, OpenAI's DALL-E, and Adobe Firefly.

Each art generator has its pros and cons. Stable Diffusion is free, but it has a significant learning curve. MidJourney's AI art generator is the most stylized, but its paid plans are expensive and its development team lacks focus. They struggle to ship new features, and the features they focus on are head-scratching (3D models, video, personality tests to fine tune the art generator, and so on). Adobe Firefly is the newest entrant in the race, but the quality of its generations doesn't yet match that of Stable Diffusion's and MidJourney's, though its generative fill features inside of Photoshop are nothing short of extraordinary. The company also promises to help defend anyone sued by copyright holders claiming the model violates their copyright.

In short, there is no clear winner yet. There are benefits and drawbacks to using each.

As things stand right now, if the MidJourney team continues in its lack of focus and ability to ship features much requested by its community, it will fall behind and/or possibly be acquired. Sometimes I think they're not serious about wanting to compete. Also, there's the problem of MidJourney potentially poisoning the well by training its models without permission from copyright holders. This may put a ceiling on MidJourney's ability to be a market leader because it cannot (like Adobe) guarantee that its work does not violate copyright.

Stable Diffusion has many of the same problems as MidJourney, though its development team is more focused.

OpenAI's DALL-e seems neglected, and it only recently received an update.

All things considered, the AI generators have their pros and cons. However, the quality of their output has taken a substantial leap forward since 2022. In fact, if you were to use the same prompt on their 2022 editions versus their 2023 editions, you would think that the outputs are from different applications entirely. The quality is increasing so quickly that it is difficult to comprehend. For example, the AI generators render people so realistically that you have to look very closely to spot if they are AI generated. And even then, you don't really know for sure. This was not the case a year ago, when the AI art generators were creating deformed faces, hands, and necks. I'd say this issue is just about fixed.

As another example, a year ago, these apps were good at creating abstract art that looked as if it had been inspired by a dream. More specific art styles like Japanese ukiyo-e or ultra photorealism, not so much. Now, these art generators can create damn near any image in any style you want. Their only limitation is whether the art generator is trained on a specific artist's work. I'd say this issue is almost solved.

The issues that AI art development teams are working on right now are higher-quality up-scales, more finely-tuned outputs, and ensuring that outputs adhere more to the user's intentions.

I have a few milestones on when I think AI art technology will achieve peak performance:

- The art generators create work that is indistinguishable from a human artist.
- They can create the same model in various poses for continuity. This has not yet been achieved.
- They can produce any output in a layered Photoshop file.
- Their in-painting feature allows users to modify any part of the AI image seamlessly and without hassle. The generators are partly there, though there is still a long way to go.

These are the milestones that need to happen in order for AI art to dominate the mainstream and step into its full potential. Gone are the days where we talk about how good and beautiful AI art images are. That milestone has been surpassed. AI art now generates images that are good enough for almost any task: blog posts, book covers, art on your wall, and so on. The problem is that while the inputs are beautiful, they do not (yet) exactly match what users are looking for. Instead, users determine what they want and are pleasantly surprised by what the AI creates. If this technology is to progress further, we must enter an era of customization where the user may not get exactly what they want, but they can get there using modification tools such as in-painting, variations, and other tools that haven't been invented yet.

I'm still bullish about the future of AI art generators, but we have arrived at a plateau. I will make a note to follow up on the status of AI art this time next year so I can further measure just how far it has come.

LOOKING FORWARD

THE GREAT AI QUIET

This past quarter, *everyone* has been talking about AI. Also this quarter, *no one* has been talking about AI.

Just so that I'm very clear, I have to separate AI art from AI text and other AI software.

For AI art, the conversation has died down considerably. Yes, there are still parties on both sides who feel very strongly in support of or against AI art, but for the most part, the battles are over. I'm not so sure that artists have come to peace with the technology so much as they have stopped venting about it publicly. Additionally, several lawsuits that began with triumphant fanfare at the beginning of the year in support of artists against companies like MidJourney and Stable Diffusion were dismissed. Companies like Adobe and OpenAI's DALL-e appear to have gotten their models on a good footing by only training them with content they had permission to use and also exploring ways to compensate media creators when their work is used in an AI art generator. It seems there are more companies taking this route than there were at the beginning of this journey, and that's encouraging. I don't quite know how artists feel about Adobe Firefly or OpenAI's DALL-e, but they are distinctly different from MidJourney and Stable Diffusion in the area of copyright permission. As these models advance and acquire more market share, the issue of models that violate copyright is lessened somewhat.

In short, I couldn't open my email or visit any social media website without hearing someone complain about AI art. Now, I don't hear the complaining nearly as much.

Four AI text, things are even quieter, but for different reasons. With the advent of AI art generators, there was much hysteria in the writing community about the impact of AI writing apps as well, though the quality of writing apps was never anywhere near as good as what AI art generators were producing. AI art generators produce stunning works of art; AI text generators, not so much. Sure, they can write simple nonfiction that approaches the quality of a human author, but they can't write fiction well. Not yet. For this reason, I believe that fears around AI writing apps were probably overblown. At the time of this writing, I can only think of one major AI writing app that produces somewhat usable results. That app is Sudowrite. But even then, Sudowrite is powered by OpenAI's GPT models, and ChatGPT is not capable of writing good fiction or nonfiction at this time.

So, things are quiet right now. Is it the quiet before the storm? I don't know, but it is an interesting observation of the current time.

THIS TIME LAST YEAR

This is a recurring segment in the *Indie Author Confidential* series in which I look back at what I was doing this time last year.

This time last year, I was doing a lot.

I finalized my dictation macro, which allowed me to dictate using my voice recorder and edit my work on the fly with my voice. That was an incredibly enabling project that exploded my word counts.

I was also celebrating the ten-year anniversary of my near-death experience and reflecting on how far I had come.

I also made some major updates to my portfolio, revamping my master publishing file, reducing the amount of links in my e-books, and making overall improvements that would make it easier for me to manage my book portfolio.

I was also learning cover design, and I still am, though I'm not making much progress at the moment...

I also experimented with a new audiobook production process that involved using AI for proofing. That was successful and will be my default process moving forward.

And finally, I also discovered Paste, my clipboard manager that saves everything I cut or copy to my clipboard. It was my favorite app I found last year, and I continue to use it every day. It saves me so much time.

It's a short but sweet summary. It's amazing how time flies.

THIS TIME FIVE YEARS AGO

Five years ago, it was 2018. What an interesting and complicated year.

I was a manager at a Fortune 100 insurance company, and I didn't like the job. I was a bad fit for it. I liked the director who hired me, but he found another job shortly after hiring me. The job was stressful and I was unprepared for it. It took a toll on my health and taught me a lot about myself.

Yet, I wrote like crazy. I published my *Dream Mage* series. It's the story of Aisha Robinson, a mage who can manipulate people's dreams. She and her cousins run a dream interpretation business where Aisha reads people's dreams in order to help them solve their problems. And of course, things always go wrong when she enters someone's mind. She's part mage, part therapist, and part action hero.

The second novel in that series, *Nightmare Stalkers,* was the most fun I've ever had writing a novel. I wrote it in seven thrilling days.

The Dream Mage series was my first urban fantasy series, and it's the series that made me want to settle down in urban fantasy. Before it, I wrote in many genres. Looking back on it, that was a critical moment in my career.

It was during this year that I mastered the art of writing on my phone; my job required me to travel a lot, so I realized that if I was going to continue being a writer, I had to learn how to write on-the-go.

I also wrote *Be a Writing Machine*, a little book that would change the course of my writing career. It boosted my nonfiction book sales and launched me into the speaking circuit. *Be a Writing Machine* was a watershed moment in my life. When I wrote the book, I had no expectations that it would sell any copies. I wrote it for myself. That ended up being the reason why it did so well.

It's hard to believe it's been five years.

THIS TIME TEN YEARS AGO

Ten years ago, I was writing my first novel, *How to Be Bad* (known now as *Magic Souls*). It was a masterclass in writing a book.

I've heard it said that your first novel encapsulates all of your hopes, dreams, and fears. Boy, was this true with *Magic Souls*!

I did just about everything wrong with the novel, but I am still proud of it because it's my first novel.

First, I had no concept of marketing. I didn't know how to communicate the book idea, or how to position it in the market.

Magic Souls follows Bebe McFerrin, an attorney who is a pushover. She can't stand up for herself. One day, after a colleague betrays her during an important presentation at work, a demon appears and offers her the ability to get revenge against her colleague. She can commit any crime and will not get caught. Bebe accepts and gets her revenge, but the demon wants help in return. He wants the souls of three innocent people, which Bebe must acquire by gaining their trust and betraying them. If Bebe doesn't go along with the plan, she'll lose her own soul.

Magic Souls is an interactive adventure styled after *Choose Your Own Adventure* novels. Unlike a traditional novel, it lets the reader decide how the story progresses. The decisions are multifaceted and complicated, and the book even has a real game show baked into it.

This type of novel is difficult to market and it sells very few copies per year. The reason is that interactive novels are a niche genre. Also, the style of interactivity used in this novel was ahead of its time and (still today) unlike anything else on the market. Most interactive novels function exactly like *Choose Your Own Adventures*, whereas the decisions in my novel are more complex and nuanced.

My process of writing *Magic Souls* was very different from how I write novels today. I wrote the novel and revised it extensively, somewhere around five drafts.

I hired a developmental editor, something I'd never do today. I had never worked with an editor before, so I had to learn how to use Word's tracked changes.

I bought a pre-made book cover, not knowing anything about what should be on a book cover. I just picked a cover that looked cool. And cool it was. Effective? Nope. But hey, it only cost me $30.

I also had to educate myself on e-book formatting. To say that formatting an interactive e-book is difficult is an understatement. I learned a lot about the technical aspects of e-books and used that knowledge to great effect. This helped me learn Scrivener at a deep level quickly, knowledge that would serve me well throughout my entire writing career.

I purchased a trademark for this book. I marketed this book as a "Decision Select" series, and I thought a trademark would be a smart idea. It was not, and it cost me dearly. I wasted every dime.

I published *Magic Souls* in Amazon's Kindle Direct

Publishing (KDP) Select, making it exclusive to Amazon for 90 days. Then, I published it widely on as many retailers as I could.

After I hit the publish button, I went on my honeymoon to Mexico. I (seriously) thought I would return home to a six-figure writing salary. The joke was on me because I sold three copies and made $5.78. The people who bought the book were me, my mom, and a writer friend. Yikes.

In almost every aspect, *Magic Souls* was a failure. But ultimately, it was a success. It was the first novel that I finished. It taught me the basics of the business. And most importantly, it gave me a taste of what was possible. It inspired me to keep going. For all of these reasons, the book was a smashing success.

I wouldn't be where I am today if it weren't for *Magic Souls*. And that's something to be grateful for.

READ THE NEXT VOLUME

Michael's writer journey continues in the next volume of this series!

Grab your copy at www.authorlevelup.com/confidential.

MEET M.L. RONN

Science fiction and fantasy on the wild side!

M.L. Ronn (Michael La Ronn) is the author of many science fiction and fantasy novels including *The Good Necromancer*, *Android X*, and *The Last Dragon Lord* series.

In 2012, a life-threatening illness made him realize that storytelling was his #1 passion. He's devoted his life to writing ever since, making up whatever story makes him fall out of his chair laughing the hardest. Every day.

Learn more about Michael
www.authorlevelup.com (for writers)
www.michaellaronn.com (fiction)

MORE BOOKS BY M.L. RONN

Books for Writers:

www.authorlevelup.com/books

Fiction:

www.michaellaronn.com/books